M000081942

PREVAILING
PRAYER

*Truths compiled
from the writings of*

FRANCIS
FRANGIPANE

*BECOMING
A HOUSE
OF PRAYER*

Scripture taken from the New American Standard Bible
© 1960, 1962, 1963, 1968, 1971, 1972, 1973, 1975, 1977
by the Lockman Foundation. Used by permission.

All rights reserved
Printed in the United States of America

ISBN #1-886296-01-4

Copyright © 1994 Francis Frangipane
Arrow Publications, Inc.
P.O. Box 10102
Cedar Rapids, IA 52410

CONTENTS

Chapters originally from *The Divine Antidote*, which is now published under the title of *The Power of Covenant Prayer* - Published by Creation House

1.

LEGAL PROTECTION

Faith is More Than Doctrines

Approximately two thousand years ago a decree was issued from the judgment seat of God. It provided "legal" protection for the church against the devil. Indeed, when Jesus died for our sins, the **"ruler of this world"** was judged; our debts were nailed to Christ's cross and cancelled, and principalities and powers were disarmed (John 16:11; Col 2:13-15). Because of Jesus, we have a legal right not only to be protected from our enemy but to triumph over him.

The sacrifice of Christ was so complete, and the judicial decision from God against Satan so decisive, that divine protection, enough to cover even the entire church in a city, has been granted (see Rev 3:10).

Christ's death is the lawful platform upon which the church rises to do spiritual warfare; His Word is the eternal sword we raise against wickedness. Having said that, we must also acknowledge that the church has only rarely walked in such victory since the first century. Why? The answer is this: *To attain the protection of Christ, the church must embrace the intercession of Christ.* We must become a house of prayer.

Indeed, church history began with its leadership devoted to the Word of God and to prayer (see Acts 2:42; 6:4). *Every day* the leaders gathered to pray and minister to the Lord (see Acts 3:1). In this clarity of vision and simplicity of purpose, the church of Jesus Christ never had greater power or capacity to make true disciples. These men and women revealed the purity of the Kingdom of God.

Today, however, our qualifications for church leadership include almost anything but devotion to God's Word and prayer. Leaders are expected to be organizers, counselors, and individuals with winning personalities whose charms alone can draw people.

In Luke 18, Jesus challenges our modern traditions. He asks, **"When the Son of Man comes, will He find faith on the earth?"** (v 8) His question is a warning to Christians who would limit the power of God at the end of the age. Jesus is calling us to resist the downward pull of our traditions; He is asking us as individuals, *"Will I find faith in you?"*

Before we respond, let us note that Jesus associates **"faith"** with **"day and night"** prayer (Luke 18:7). He is not asking, *"Will I find correct doctrines in you?"* The Lord's question does not so much concern itself with right knowledge as with right faith. *What* we believe is important, but *how* we believe is vital in securing the help of God.

Indeed, procuring the supernatural help of God is exactly the point of Jesus' parable in Luke 18. His intent was to show that **"at all times"** we **"ought to pray and not to lose heart"** (Luke 18:1). To illustrate the quality of faith He seeks, He followed His admonition with a parable about a certain widow who petitioned a hardened judge for **"legal protection"** (v 3). Although the judge was initially unwilling, yet by her **"continually coming"** (v 5) she gained what was legally hers.

Jesus concluded by saying if an unrighteous judge will respond to a widow's persistence, shall not God avenge quickly **"His elect, who cry to Him day and night, and will He delay long over them?"** Jesus said, **"I tell you that He will bring about justice for them speedily"** (see Luke 18:1-8).

Understanding God's Delays

Our Heavenly Judge will not delay long over His elect, but He *will* delay. In fact, God's definition of "speedily" and ours are not always synonymous. The Lord incorporates delays into His overall plan: They work perseverance in us. So crucial is endurance to our character development that God is willing to delay even important answers to prayer to facilitate our transformation.

Thus, we should not interpret divine delays as signs of divine reluctance. Delays are tools to perfect our faith. Christ is looking to find a tenacity in our faith that prevails in spite of delays and setbacks. He seeks to create a perseverance within us that outlasts the test of time, a resolve that *actually grows stronger* during delays. When the Father sees this quality of persistence in our faith, it so touches His heart that He grants **"legal protection"** to His people.

Desperation Produces Change

It is significant that Jesus compared His elect to a widow harassed by an enemy. The image is actually liberating, for we tend to conceptualize the heroes of the faith as David or Joshua types—individuals whose successes obscure their humble beginnings. But each of God's servants has, like the widow, a former life that is brimming with excuses and occasions to waver.

Look at the widow: She has legitimate reasons to quit, but instead she prevails. Indeed, she refuses to exempt herself from her high potential simply because of her low estate. She makes no apologies for her lack of finances, knowledge, or charm. Giving herself no reason to fail, she unashamedly plants her case before the judge where she pleads for and receives what is hers: legal protection from her opponent.

How did a common widow gain such strength of character? We can imagine that there must have been a time when, under the relentless pressure of her adversary, she became desperate—and desperation worked to her advantage. Desperation is God's hammer: It demolishes the stronghold of fear and shatters the chains of our excuses. When desperation exceeds our fears, progress begins.

Today, the force prodding many Christians toward greater unity and prayer has not been the sweetness of fellowship; more often it has been the assault of the enemy. We are in desperate times. When it comes to touching God's heart, other than for a few essential truths, unity of desperation is more crucial than unity of doctrine.

Consider the degree of our national moral decline: In the time it takes to read this chapter, ten babies will be aborted in America. Based on current statistics, this year there will be an estimated 34 million crimes committed. Of those, nearly 600,000 will be violent crimes, and 72% of that number will be against our *teenagers*. In what place is a teen most frequently assaulted, raped, or murdered today? Most violent acts are committed against teens in their schools!

God's Elect

Our nation is suffering from a deep social and moral collapse. If we have ever needed God's anointing, it is now—but where are God's elect? Where are the people whom Daniel says **"know their God,"** and **"will display strength and take action"?** (Dan 11:32)

Is there no one divinely empowered who can fell the Goliaths of our age? Perhaps we are looking in the wrong places. Perhaps we need only to look in our bathroom mirror. If you believe in Jesus and are desperate for God, you qualify as one of God's elect. Remember, in the above parable the *widow* typifies Christ's chosen.

We have erroneously held that God's chosen will never be assaulted by the adversary, much less driven to desperation and "day and night" prayer. But, this desperation is often the very crucible in which the elect of God are forged. Jesus portrays this characteristic metaphorically in the picture of the widow; He reveals the means through which His elect prevail in battle at the end of the age.

When all is said and done, it is also possible that this widow may not have been a singular person, but a corporate people—a "widow church"—united in Christ in a singular, desperate prayer for protection against her adversary.

We need the "legal protection" that a national revival provides. But it will not come without unceasing prayer. You ask, "Where was the prayer behind the Charismatic Renewal?" The Lord spoke to my heart that the Charismatic Renewal was His answer to the cries of a million praying mothers—women who refused to surrender their children to drugs and the devil.

It is our turn to pray; we are the widow who cannot give herself a reason for failure. God will answer our day and night cry. Let us position ourselves at His throne. Certainly, He will grant us legal protection in our cities.

Heavenly Father, forgive us for our lack of prayer and for giving ourselves excuses to fail. Lord, we thank You for making us desperate. Help us now to prevail, to attain the "legal protection" You have provided us against our adversary. In Jesus' name. Amen.

2.

DAY AND NIGHT PRAYER

God has provided a divine antidote for every ill in the human condition; that remedy is Jesus Christ. When we see a need or a wound in the soul of our communities, we must apply Christ as the cure.

The spiritual immunity God provides us as individuals has a divinely inspired, built-in limitation: *The Spirit of Christ which shelters us from the enemy also makes us vulnerable to the needs of others.* As it is written, **"If one member suffers, all the members suffer with it"** (1 Cor 12:26). Thus, to perfect love, God unites us to other people; and to empower prayer, He allows us to be vicariously identified with the sufferings of those we care for.

If we cease to love, we will fail to pray. Love is the fuel behind all intercession. Are you weary or vacillating in your prayer life? Remember the love God first gave you, whether it is for your family or church, city or nation. Love will identify you with those you love; it will revive your prayer, and prayer will revive your loved ones.

Consider Daniel. Daniel loved Israel. He loved the temple. Although Daniel was not guilty of the sins of Israel, his prayer was an expression of his identification with the nation. Daniel put on sackcloth and ashes and sought the Lord with prayer and supplication. He prayed,

> **"Alas, O Lord, the great and awesome God, who keeps His covenant and lovingkindness for those who love Him and keep His commandments, we have sinned, committed iniquity, acted wickedly, and rebelled, even turning aside from Thy commandments and ordinances"** (Dan 9:4-5).

Had Daniel sinned? No. But his love and identification with Israel made his repentance legitimate. Additionally, Daniel was faithful in his daily prayer for Israel— he prayed all his life for the restoration of the nation. Consider: After a year or two, our faithfulness begins to wane. But Daniel was faithful every day throughout his life!

When Darius passed a law forbidding petitions to any god or man other than himself, Daniel was not intimidated. We read,

Now when Daniel knew that the writing was signed, he went home. And in his upper room, with his windows open toward Jerusalem, he knelt down on his knees three times that day, and prayed and gave thanks before his God, as was his custom since early days (Dan 6:10 NKJV).

Daniel was one of the first exiles from Israel to Babylon. We can imagine, in the terror and trauma of seeing one's society destroyed and its survivors enslaved and exiled, that Daniel's parents had firmly planted in his young heart Solomon's prayer, which embodied God's requirements for restoration:

"When Thy people Israel are defeated before an enemy, because they have sinned against Thee, if they turn to Thee again and confess Thy name and pray and make supplication to Thee in this house, then hear Thou in heaven, and forgive the sin of Thy people Israel, and bring them back to the land which Thou didst give to their fathers" (1 Kings 8:33-34).

Thus, Daniel prayed three times a day, every day, since his earliest years. He continued in prayer for nearly *seventy years*, until the time Jeremiah's prophecy came to pass!

You see, the work of God takes time. How long should we pray? We pray as long as it takes. Consider Anna, who ministered to the Lord in prayer and fasting in the temple for approximately *sixty years*, crying out to God until He sent the Messiah. Or, Cornelius, whose **"prayers and alms . . . ascended as a memorial before God"** (Acts 10:4). We do not understand the responsibility and privilege God places upon a person who continues in faithful prayer. What sustained these champions of prayer? They loved God and loved the people of God.

Costly Lessons

While the work of revival is often initiated through the love and intercession of one person, there is a time when the prayer burden must be picked up and shared by many. It is not enough that God graces one individual to become a man or woman of prayer; the Lord seeks to make His church a house of prayer.

One way or another, the plan of God is to make intercessors of us all. We can learn the indispensable priority of prayer directly from God's Word. We can also learn of the need to pray from the victories or mistakes of others. Or, we can learn of the necessity of prayer the hard way: We can fail to pray and let the consequences teach us.

For some, these will be costly lessons. And, we will not be able to blame the devil if the *real* culprit was our neglect of prayer. In extreme cases, the Lord will actually allow tragedy to reinforce the urgency and priority of prayer. The following incident from the book of Acts underscores the need to keep our prayer life strong and sensitive to changes in our spiritual battles. The story also reveals that tremendous power is released when the whole church in a city prays.

Of all Jesus' followers, three were considered the "inner circle": Peter, James, and John. Yet, Luke tells us of a terrible event in the life of the early Christians: Herod executed the apostle James. Until that time the leaders of the church walked in spiritual protection. However, they failed to discern that the intensity of satanic assault had escalated. The result was that James, an apostle who stood with Christ on the Mount of Transfiguration, was beheaded.

The appalling murder of James shocked the Church. How was it that this anointed apostle died so prematurely? Where was God's protection? Perhaps this is the answer: The Lord suppressed His *sovereign protection* that He might bring the church into *intercessory protection.*

The death of James pleased the Jews, so Herod imprisoned Peter also, intending to kill him after the Feast of Unleavened Bread. At this point, the Scripture says, **"Peter therefore was kept in prison; but prayer was made without**

ceasing of the church unto God for him" (Acts 12:5 KJV). The New King James Version says that **"constant prayer"** was offered to God; the New International Version says the church was praying **"earnestly"**; the New American Standard Bible tells us that the church was praying **"fervently."** *Earnest, fervent, constant prayer was made for Peter by the entire church in Jerusalem!*

The outcome of this aggressive intercession was that Peter was supernaturally delivered, the guards who held Peter were executed, and, a short time later, Herod himself was struck down by an angel of the Lord. *When the entire citywide church engaged in continual, day and night prayer, God granted deliverance!*

In the many years I have served the Lord, I have known individuals, prayer groups, and even denominations which have embraced varying degrees of 24-hour prayer. I have participated with prayer chains and prayer vigils. But I have yet to see an entire, citywide Christian community put aside minor doctrinal differences and take God's promise seriously.

When the local churches in a community truly become a house united in prayer, God will begin to guide the entire church into the shelter of His protection. And, according to Jesus, **"He will bring about justice for them speedily"** (Luke 18:8).

Lord God, restore us to Your love. Your Word says that love never fails. Master, we know that we have failed often; we faint because we lose sight of love. Master, by Your grace, we purpose to identify those people that we love and then to be faithful in prayer until You touch them. We also purpose to follow Your leading until all the Christians in the city are crying to You in prayer. Help us, Father, to discern the priority of prayer. In Jesus' name. Amen.

3.

REPENTANCE PRECEDES REVIVAL

A true revival does not just happen. There are conditions which must reside in the human heart before the Lord visits His people.

We Must Want Deliverance, Not Just Relief

Too often, ministries today seek to deliver people who are unwilling to repent of sins, who have not cried in their heart to God for help. The effect is that those prayed for may receive limited relief, but they soon fall back into sin and oppression. The key to successful deliverance is to discern if an individual is *ready* and *will-*

ing to be released before we minister deliverance. Are they repentant? Have they put away their idols? Is their heart truly turning toward God?

God's pattern for us as individuals is also His pattern for the church and the city. Even as the Lord did not deliver us until we cried for help, so the war for our churches and cities will not be won until a significant number of us are crying to God in prayer. Christ's purpose in bringing the citywide church to prayer is to provide the proper heart attitudes to which the Almighty can respond.

Without the substructure of prayer and crying before God, deliverance, "binding and loosing," and other forms of spiritual warfare are significantly limited. Deliverance, according to Scripture, is the last stage of a process that began when a person's abhorrence for his present condition led him to cry to God for help.

The Deliverers

The Old Testament reveals God's pattern for deliverance and revival: In answer to the prayers and sufferings of His people, the Lord raised up deliverers. They were individuals who were anointed and empowered by God to defeat Israel's oppressors.

It is important to note that the effectiveness of these deliverers was never based upon their own worthiness or credentials. While they were uniquely sent by God, their arrival was synchronized with Israel's repentance. No repentance; no deliverance. As Israel cried to God, the deliverers were commissioned and anointed with the power of the Holy Spirit.

The essence of this Old Testament pattern for renewal can be applied to us in our day. We may not see actual "deliverers" as much as we will see revival emerge in those cities where prayer and repentance is deep and widespread.

Again, looking at the Israel model: National sin brought defeat and dominance by foreign powers. With foreign domination came the worship of demons and the complete seduction of Israel's heart by the enemy. As Israel blatantly defied God's laws, so came the economic, cultural, and physical collapse of the nation. Where once the people enjoyed the blessing of God, now despair and misery dwelt upon the land.

It was in this context of suffering, of people genuinely and deeply crying to God, that the Lord raised up deliverers. These individuals led a *repentant* Israel into victory over their oppressors. As true worship was established, national peace and prosperity followed.

It should be noted that the route to revival was not set according to a timetable; it was not precisely scheduled. No one can forecast how long judgment will last nor when repentance has so excavated the heart of sinful man that God is satisfied. This one fact is true: *The time it takes will always be longer than we expect.* The determining factors are the acknowledgement of sin and the return to God. Once the nation was securely turned toward God, healing for their land soon followed.

Nehemiah speaks of this pattern of repentance preceding national deliverance. He prayed,

> **"Therefore Thou didst deliver them into the hand of their oppressors who oppressed them, but when they cried to Thee in the time of their distress, Thou didst hear from heaven, and according to Thy great compassion Thou didst give them deliverers who delivered them from the hand of their oppressors"** (Neh 9:27).

We must not hurry this process, nor be frustrated if our prayers do not immediately activate divine intervention. The Lord is waiting for the nation to break beneath the weight of its rebellion. Yet, in this we should be encouraged: Our intercession is the first fruits of what is destined to become a national response to the Almighty!

There may be, at times, flurries of spiritual activity, but before a national revival will come, there will be a nation crying to God. This period is called **"the time of their distress,"** and it is not consummated in revival until the nation has been crying unto the Lord for a number of years.

Man's Misery, God's Heart

In the book of Judges this pattern occurs time and again. While Israel tumbled deeper into sin, God waited for the burden and consequences of Israel's sin to humble their souls. He waited to bring them back to Himself.

Yet, the Lord was not aloof from Israel's sorrows. Even when they were in rebellion, He felt their sufferings. When the Lord **"could bear the misery of Israel no longer"** (Judg 10:16), He sent them deliverers. *The misery and desperation of Israel readied them for God.*

We see this pattern in Exodus in the Lord's encounter with Moses. The Redeemer said,

> **"I have surely seen the affliction of My people who are in Egypt, and have given heed to their cry because of their taskmasters, for I am aware of their sufferings. So I have come down to deliver them"** (Ex 3:7-8).

Notice the Lord *saw* the affliction of His people, He *heard* their cries, He *knew* their sufferings. God is never far from the plight of mankind. In truth, He bears the misery of our society: Our distresses distress Him; our suffering becomes His sorrow.

Returning to our text in Exodus, observe also that it was not merely their prayers which God heard; He heard their *cries.* It is one thing to pray about a need, quite another to weep over it. It is those who *mourn* whom God comforts.

The Lord knew their afflictions and their sufferings. The prayer to which God responds is a constant cry, often born out of "afflictions" and "sufferings," as in the former Soviet Union and parts of Africa and Asia.

Perhaps the Lord has not fully answered us because our prayers are still comfortably contained within a schedule. As we stated earlier, the Charismatic Renewal began in the constant "day and night" cry of a million mothers. This was not the result of a mere hour of prayer; it emerged out of the continual cry of mothers (and fathers) who were deeply troubled about their children. Their prayer was not a religious discipline; it was the heart-throb of their existence. Without the sophisticated machinery of spiritual warfare, the tears and weeping of their unceasing intercession prevailed before God, and He rescued their children.

Perhaps what delays revival in our times is that we are troubled, but we are not *afflicted* by the conditions of our society; though saddened, we are not yet *weeping*. It must be acknowledged, however, that a growing number of God's people have truly surrendered to the vulnerability of Christ's compassions. They bear in their intercessions not only the needs of the people, but the pains of the people as well. They are laying down their reputations, their jobs, yes, even their lives to see the sins of our society cleansed.

Although still a minority, these intercessors carry in their souls the anguish of their cities. They hear the cry of the oppressed; they know the suffering of both the unborn and the born. God is ready to respond to their prayer. Out of the womb of their distress, God shall bring forth deliverance.

The praying church should not limit the length of its dedication to intercession. God is looking for a *life* of prayer, not just a *season*. If the duration of time required to bring change can stop us, it is obvious that the preparatory work in our hearts is not deep enough to draw divine intervention.

How does all this relate to revival? Spiritual renewal *is* the divine antidote for our cities and our nation. It is God's answer to all who cry unceasingly to Him for help.

Lord, forgive us for wanting relief instead of deliverance, for looking for shortcuts instead of Your perfect will. Master, we know that Your heart cannot refuse the genuine cry of the afflicted, that You cannot long bear the misery of Your people without acting on our behalf. So, we cry to You today! Send the rain of Your Presence back to us! Cleanse us from our lusts for comfort and apathy. Bring us to the place where You can honor Your integrity and bring revival to our land! For Your glory we pray. Amen.

4.

SENT BY GOD

Deliverance for our nation is coming, and we have written about the fundamental conditions which precipitate revival. However, it is important to identify the nature of those whom God sends, lest the enemy plant counterfeit ministries and the move of God stalls. To give us a general overview of the spiritual traits the Lord works in His servant, we will study the life of Gideon.

Let us recall that deliverers were raised up when evil and oppression covered the land. Although instrumental in bringing great light and prosperity to Israel, the ministry of deliverance was always birthed out of a womb of social darkness and trauma.

"Now it came about when the sons of Israel cried to the Lord on account of Midian, that the Lord sent a pro-

phet" (Judg 6:7-8). Once again, we see that the future deliverance of Israel began with the sons of Israel crying to the Lord.

The Lord responded to the Jews with a prophetic word. The prophetic anointing does more than teach; it proclaims the intention of God. It also confronts strongholds of sin in the people and prepares society for an outpouring of the Spirit.

In this case, the prophet was not the deliverer; he simply reminded Israel of former deliverances. He reiterated God's command of many generations: **"I am the Lord your God; you shall not fear the gods of the Amorites in whose land you live"** (v 10).

The **"gods of the Amorites"** were the demonic principalities and powers which ruled the countries in Canaan. There is an interaction between the powers of darkness and the sins of a society. When Israel was in obedience to God, the Spirit of God ruled the heavenly places over Israel. When the Jews were in rebellion, the enemy gained control of the nation through the sins of the people. Evil ruled in the spiritual realms over Israel.

The idols erected to these evil spirits were physical symbols of spiritual bondage. Paul instructs us that when people sacrifice to an idol, **"they sacrifice to demons"** (1 Cor 10:20). However, the Lord commanded Israel not to fear these demon-gods. The Hebrew word for "fear" means "to reverence; to live in an intellectual or emotional anticipation of harm." We will never be victorious over the enemy if we fear his retaliation.

It must be stated that it is great wisdom to not move presumptuously in spiritual warfare. No one should be flippant or casual against powers of darkness. Yet, it is a greater error to be afraid of the enemy. Satan does, indeed, have a "right" to occupy the spiritual realms of sin and rebellion. However, we are commanded not to fear the "gods of the Amorites" or, in our case, the "principalities and powers" over our cities.

If a Christian teacher instructs you to fear principalities and powers, you must not fear what he fears. You should respect the power of the enemy, but it is sin to live in fear of these demons. Israel spent forty years in the wilderness because they feared when they saw giants in the land of promise. The Lord has given us authority over all the power of the enemy; He promises, **"Nothing shall injure you"** (Luke 10:19).

The Man is the Plan

The prophet rebuked Israel for fearing the gods of the Canaanites. The Lord then set Himself to deliver Israel of fear. God always begins the deliverance of the many with the deliverance of one, and so He sought out Gideon.

The angel of the Lord found Gideon hiding from the Midianites. His greeting was astounding: **"The Lord is with you, O valiant warrior"** (Judg 6:12).

Although the years of preparation might be many, when the Lord unsheathes His sword, He moves quickly. God wasted no time in establishing the man of His choosing, calling him by his future identity: *valiant warrior.*

Gideon, no doubt, wondered that he was the valiant warrior to whom the angel spoke. And this is the first aspect of those whom God intends to use: *He is surprised, even shocked, that the Lord has called him!* He has no secret wish to be a hero; no hidden ambition for prominence. He is not even a "natural born" leader.

We might imagine that, in Gideon's fear, he concluded there was another person, a **"valiant warrior,"** near him of whom he was unaware. There is a Valiant Warrior in us whom we, too, are often unaware. His name is the Lord of Hosts, and greater is He who is in us than he who is in the world.

In this first encounter, Gideon asked the Lord a very legitimate question, **"If the Lord is with us, why then has all this happened to us? . . . where are all His miracles?"** (Judg 6:13) This is a question that everyone who sincerely seeks the endorsement of God must ask. Why does it seem as though the Lord has abandoned us? We must know why there seems to be a distance between the Lord and our need so we can repent and be restored.

However, God had not left His people. The question is actually superfluous, for if the Lord initiated this encounter with Gideon, then the time of separation had past; the time of His visitation was at hand.

"And the Lord looked at him and said, 'Go in this your strength and deliver Israel from the hand of Midian. Have I not sent you?' " (v 14). Gideon was the youngest in his father's house, and his family was the least in Manasseh. What strength had he? How could Gideon deliver Israel? The strength of God's servants is in their commission from the Lord. This is the next aspect of a true servant of God: *Having been sent by God, he goes in divine authority.*

Let us remember that Jesus gave His disciples the same appointment Gideon received, **"As Thou didst send Me into the world, I also have sent them into the world"** (John 17:18). The commission of the Lord carries the endorsement of the Lord; He will back with power those whom He sends!

At this point Gideon's eyes were opened and He saw God. Concerned about his own unworthiness, he cried out, **"Alas, O Lord God! For now I have seen the angel of the Lord face to face"** (Judg 6:22). But the Lord said to him, **"Peace to you, do not fear; you shall not die"** (v 23).

Gideon built an altar to the Lord and called it, **"The Lord is Peace"** (v 24). No one can truly stand against the enemy if they are unsure of their standing before God. And this is the third qualification for those whom God sends: *He has peace with*

God. Before the Lord sends His servants forth, they must know the power of His blood, the forgiveness of their sins, and their justification by faith. Whenever they look toward heaven, they must know **"The Lord is Peace."**

Ourselves, Our Families and Our Cities!

The Lord said,

"Pull down the altar of Baal which belongs to your father, and cut down the Asherah that is beside it; and build an altar to the Lord your God on the top of this stronghold in an orderly manner" (Judg 6:25-26).

The same night the Lord revealed Himself to Gideon, He sent him to pull down the altar of Baal and also to cut down the Asherah. Now, although the altar to Baal was in the center of town, it belonged to Gideon's father. There is a sequence here worth noting. After the Lord delivered Gideon, He sent him to pull down the strongholds in his family.

This is the fourth aspect of the nature of those whom the Lord sends: *They are anointed to bring order.* Generally speaking, that order begins with their own families. Their homes may not be perfect, but they will be in order. God is very concerned with all the *dis*order in the church. Those whom God sends initiate reconciliation and repentance. Because they are individuals who are filled with the grace and truth of Christ, their influence is greatly respected. But, the process of bringing order starts in the little, non-public relationships of their own homes.

We encourage each of you to begin the battle for your city by pulling down the strongholds in your home. Bring your family into prayer, and through prayer, bring healing and order. If you fail in this preparation, the enemy will always have open doors to counterattack and undermine your credibility (see 1 Tim 3:5).

It is also important to note that pulling down a stronghold is only half the battle; on that very site we must now build an altar to the Lord. For example, if the stronghold was fear, it must be replaced with an altar of faith. If bitterness existed, love must take its place. On a citywide scale, where perversion once ruled, purity must now reign; where greed was master, generosity must preside.

Gideon pulled down his father's altar to Baal, and instead of being welcomed and applauded by the people of Ophah, they came en masse to kill him! The demonic power that ruled the area stirred its captives to fight against the Lord's servant! Gideon's father defended his son, however, and said, **"If he** [Baal] **is a god, let him contend for himself"** (Judg 6:31). Be aware: There will be those whose thoughts are so sympathetic with the very evil God has sent you to destroy, that they will rise up in defense of the devil! Expect resistance, even among God's people!

The Lord used Gideon to mobilize a large army, which the Lord promptly reduced to 300 soldiers. It is important to note that, in the process of restoration, it will never seem like God has given us enough people or skills to accomplish the task. This lack, however, is made up by God. And perhaps this is the last characteristic of those whom God anoints: *Having been sent by the Lord with His purpose, they ultimately mobilize God's people to face their enemies and conquer them.*

Significantly, Gideon was renamed "Jerubbaal," which meant "Contender with Baal." In the Bible, whenever there was a name change, there was a change of nature as well. Gideon went from being a fearful captive to a fearless warrior.

In summary, in answer to the prayers and cries of His people, a new anointing is coming. Throughout the nations we see individuals laying down their lives, drawing the church together in repentance and prayer. From among these will come the power to guide their churches and cities into revival.

They will be sent by God. They will not come to "try" anything; they will come to carry out the expressed purpose of God. What they decree will come to pass. They will lead a repentant people out of oppression and into God's remedy for their cities: Revival!

Father, draw your people together to pray, to feel and to absorb into their souls the desperate condition of their cities. Lord, as Isaiah said, "Here am I, send me." Forgive me for fearing the enemy. Lord, bring Your anointing to Your servants that, through Your power, we might see our nation turned back to You. In Jesus' name. Amen.

Notes

5.

COVENANT POWER

It is right to pray for the Lord to bless and protect our lives. However, praying for the blessing and provision of God is not the same as covenanting with Him. *A covenant is an altar upon which the Lord and His covenant partner give themselves fully to each other.*

A covenant relationship with God does not cease once our prayers have been answered. For, in covenant love we mature from simply being "believers" in prayer to becoming living sacrifices, given to God's highest plans. By so yielding, He creates within us a life that He can use extraordinarily in the process of divine redemption.

Covenant power is greater than that which comes through prayer alone. Indeed, the effects of a covenant reach far beyond simple faith. Prayer and faith are essentials; they are prerequisites, but not substitutes, for covenant power.

Thus, a covenant relationship is a life-long pledge, an unbreakable oath which God Himself initiates and promises to sustain. Contained within His promise is His unalterable commitment not only to fulfill His highest plan of redemption but to also supply grace and faith to His human counterpart along the way. Together, the All-Sufficient God and a believing man accomplish the impossible through their covenant relationship.

Power Released in a Covenant

A covenant with God accomplishes two interconnected goals. It thrusts us beyond "subjective prayer" (prayer made primarily for our personal needs) and brings us into a deeper commitment to God. Out of greater commitment comes greater grace to accomplish God's redemptive work in the world.

An example of covenant power is seen in ancient Israel during the revival which occurred after Athaliah, an idolatrous Judean queen, was dethroned. Jehoiada, the high priest, looked to God in covenant prayer. We read, **"Then Jehoiada made a covenant between the Lord and the king and the people, that they should be the Lord's people"** (2 Kings 11:17).

Did not Israel already have a covenant with God through Moses? Yes, but it is a biblical practice that individuals at various times made special covenants with the Almighty. The result of Jehoiada's covenant was that grace came upon the people and they cleansed the land of idolatry. We read, **"So all the people of the land rejoiced and the city was quiet"** (v 20). Jehoiada's covenant brought the nation back to God and ended violence in Jerusalem!

Consider also the power released in Hezekiah's covenant with the Lord. The nation of Judah had been fully corrupted by Ahaz, the preceding king. However, Hezekiah began his reign by seeking God's highest favor. He opened the doors of the temple and reconsecrated the priests.

Yet, the purification of priests and buildings would not have brought about revival had not Hezekiah taken one further step. He said, **"Now it is in my heart to make a covenant with the Lord God of Israel, that His burning anger may turn away from us"** (2 Chron 29:10). Just eight days after the king made a covenant with the Lord, we read, **"Then Hezekiah and all the people rejoiced over what God had prepared for the people, because the thing came about suddenly"** (v 36).

The difference between a long-term struggle to bring a nation around and a speedy recovery was in the power released when the king covenanted with the Almighty. Keep in mind that Judah was *apostate* in its religious practices, witchcraft was practiced by the former king, and demonic idols had been placed in the Holy of

Holies. Yet, covenant power triggered a national revival.

As Americans, it is vital we remember that our spiritual forefathers were a people who knew and exercised principles of covenant sacrifice. When the Puritans came to this country, they knelt on its shores and *covenanted* with God for this land. They dedicated this "new world" to Christ and His kingdom. It is unlikely that the revival of our nation will come without local and national church leaders covenanting together with God for the redemption of America.

Covenants with God for Our Times

A personal covenant with God is a serious commitment, worthy of extended prayer and waiting before God. At Christ's bidding, I have covenanted with Him to see the body of Christ delivered of carnal divisions and racism, that Christ's prayer of John, chapter 17, may be answered.

What does this covenant signify to me? It means that my life is not my own. It has been absorbed into something much more powerful: the will of God. It also means that when I pray, there is a power attached to my intercession that demands strongholds of religious and cultural pride to fall before God's purposes.

I have also united my life and faith with the covenants of our pilgrim forefathers. Together with a number of other brethren, both locally and nationally, we have covenanted with the Almighty to see this land restored according to 2 Chronicles 7:14.

There will be a time when this nation, like all nations, becomes the kingdom of our Lord and of His Christ (Rev 11:15). Until then, whether revival comes quickly or we pass through the fires of divine judgments, our lives belong to Christ—not simply to be blessed or made prosperous, but to see His highest purposes accomplished in our land.

Not all of us will covenant with God for the nation. Some will unite with the Lord for their families. Others will covenant with God to see abortion ended in their cities. Still others will make a covenant with God for the church, to see the Lord's House built in their cities.

Making a covenant with God takes us further into our goal of Christlikeness. It is the highest relationship we can enjoy with God; it is that which brings Him the most pleasure. To those who covenant with God, He says, **"Gather My godly ones to Me, those who have made a covenant with Me by sacrifice"** (Ps 50:5).

Lord, open our hearts to the joy and wonder, the sobriety and fear of a covenant relationship with You. Lead us, O King, out of the superficial and into the supernatural. Lead us into a covenant with You for our times and nation! In Jesus' name. Amen.

BOOKS BY FRANCIS FRANGIPANE

CALL FOR QUANTITY DISCOUNTS ON 10+ BOOKS!

This Day We Fight

Published by Chosen Books. In this day of advancing evil, will the Church wake up and fight?

Francis Frangipane tells us that the call of God is a call to war. As we stand at the cusp of a major spiritual awakening in our land, the Holy Spirit is ready to impart a fresh anointing to God's people – an anointing that will activate the "war mode" in your heart.

#FF1-027 retail $13.00 our price $10.00

The Three Battlegrounds

Revised Edition - An in-depth view of three arenas of spiritual warfare: the mind, the church and the heavenly places.

#FF2-001 retail $11.75 our price $10.00

Holiness, Truth and the Presence of God

A penetrating study of the human heart and how God prepares it for His glory.

#FF1-002 our price $9.00

The Days of His Presence

Published by Kingdom Publishing. As the day of the Lord draws near, though darkness covers the earth, the out-raying of Christ's Presence shall arise and appear upon His people!

#FF2-021 retail $11.00 our price $9.00

The House of the Lord

Published by Creation House. Pleads God's case for a Christlike church as the only hope for our cities. It takes a citywide church to win the citywide war.

#FF1-004 retail $10.00 our price $9.00

A House United

Published by Chosen Books. This is a new release of the book *It's Time to End Church Splits*.

Few works of the enemy are as destructive to the Body of Christ as a church split. Once a wedge is driven into the heart of a congregation, the result is usually bitterness, grief, even hatred among those who are called to live together in love. This new edition, has been somewhat revised. A new final section, which includes three chapters, has been added.

#FF2-026 retail: $12.00 our price: $ 9.50

The Stronghold of God

Published by Creation House. A road map into the shelter of the Most High. The atmosphere of thanksgiving, praise, faith and love are places of immunity for God's servant.

#FF2-009 retail $13.00 our price $7.80

The Power of Covenant Prayer

Published by Creation House. Takes the reader to a position of victory over witchcraft and curses. A must for those serious about attaining Christlikeness.

#FF2-010 retail $10.00 our price $9.00

The Power of One Christlike Life

Published by Whitaker House. The prayer of a Christlike intercessor is the most powerful force in the universe, delaying God's wrath until He pours out His mercy.

#FF1-025 retail $12.00 our price $7.50

To order, go to **www.arrowbookstore.com**
or call toll free (US only): **877-363-6889**
Prices subject to change

DISCIPLESHIP TRAINING BOOKLETS

(10+ AT 40%, 100+ AT 50% DISCOUNT)

COMPILED/FORMATTED FOR GROUP STUDY BY FRANCIS FRANGIPANE

Discerning of Spirits

Chapters: The Gift of Discernment; Eliminating False Discernment; Discerning the Nature of the Enemy; The Stronghold of Christ's Likeness.

#FF1-018 $4.65

The Jezebel Spirit

Chapters: Discerning the Spirit of Jezebel; Elijah, Jehu and the War Against Jezebel; Our Experience with Jezebel; Strategy Against the Spirit of Jezebel; Free to Laugh

#FF1-019 $4.65

Prevailing Prayer

Chapters: Legal Protection; Day and Night Prayer; Sent by God; Repentance Precedes Revival; Covenant Power

#FF1-011 $4.65

Overcoming Fear!

by Denise Frangipane

Testimony & Keys to Releasing the Power of Faith.   #DF1-003 $4.65

Exposing the Accuser of the Brethren

Chapters: Exposing the Accuser; Casting Down the Accuser; Protected from the Accuser; At the Throne with God

#FF1-017 $4.65

A bestseller on how to protect yourself and prosper in the midst of battle.

A Time to Seek God

Chapters: The Tent of Meeting; Two Things, Two Things Only; Unrelenting Love; Drawing Near to the Holy God; A Place for Him to Rest; The Way into the Holy Place

#FF1-020 $3.95

Deliverance from PMS

by Denise Frangipane

Practical and Spiritual Helps Toward Deliverance from PMS.   #DF1-002 $3.95

AUDIO ALBUMS

MESSAGE OF THE MONTH ANNUAL U.S. SUBSCRIPTION IS $49.00 (PLUS $ 9 SHIPPING)

Please visit www.arrowbookstore.com for a complete listing.

Jezebel Spirit

#1FF5-041   6 tapes $36.00
#2FF-041 6 CDs $36.00

The War Mode

#2FF-001 4 CDs $24.00

Pulling Down Strongholds

#1FF5-040   4 tapes $24.00
#2FF- 040 4 CDs $24.00

Walk with Integrity

#1FF5-1201 4 tapes $24.00
#2FF-1201 4 CDs $24.00

Victory Over Pain

#2FF-002 4 CDs $24.00

Writers Workshop

#WW-002   6 tapes $36.00
#WW-001 6 CDs $36.00

To order, go to **www.arrowbookstore.com**
(see complete resource catalog, current teachings, and conference schedule)
or contact **Arrow Publications, Inc.,** P.O. Box 10102, Cedar Rapids, IA 52410
Phone 1.319.395.7833 or Toll Free 1.877.363.6889 Fax 1.319.395.7353
(VISA/MC/AMERICAN EXPRESS/DISCOVER)

Call for shipping rates and quantity discounts on 10+ books!
Prices subject to change

IN CHRIST'S IMAGE TRAINING MATERIALS

Basic Training Manuals

Study series which pulls together four key areas of this ministry: Christlikeness, Humility, Prayer and Unity. Perfect for leadership teams, prayer groups, Bible studies and individuals who are seeking to possess a more Christlike life. It is strongly recommended that these four manuals be read in sequence, as each study is built upon the truths found in the preceding manuals.

#BT-001   set of 4 - retail $48.00

our price $44.00

IN CHRIST'S IMAGE TRAINING

Online Correspondence Course

Curriculum developed by
Francis Frangipane

IN CHRIST'S IMAGE TRAINING offers four opportunities for enrollment in Level I training each year: January, April, July and October.

Level I: Certification offers four foundational tracks: Christlikeness, Humility, Prayer and Unity. Completion time is six months.

Level II: Leadership Training offers further online teaching by Pastor Francis and other national church leaders. Completion time is three months.

Level III: Facilitation and Commissioning provides spiritual equipping for those preparing for ministerial opportunities.

On-site Impartation and Focused Training offers a three day seminar which can be taken by attendance or via audio tapes. For details watch our website.

Association Graduate students who desire ongoing association with other ICIT graduates, as well as fellowship with other like-minded Christians and churches, are invited to become part of Advancing Church Ministries Association of Churches and Ministries.

In Christ's Image Training center is not a denomination, nor is Advancing Church Ministries (ACM).

Please see our website at www.ICITC.org for enrollment fees and detailed information. 1-319-395-7617, training@inchristsimage.org